Statue of Liberty

Beacon of Promise

by L.E. Bond

Designed by Adine Maron
Text by L.E. Bond
Edited by Lucinda Ronyecz and Marie L. Hathaway
Editorial and Production Assistance by Angela Tripp
Typeset by Graphic Traffic, Santa Barbara, California
Printed in Hong Kong, 1st printing June 1990

ISBN 0-917859-62-6

Inside front cover: Originally christened Liberty Enlightening the World, *the Statue of Liberty was designed to stand within direct sight of passengers entering New York Harbor through the Verrazano Narrows.*

Title page: A massive 23' 7" long and 13' 7" wide, the tablet, with July 4, 1776 written in roman numerals, represents the rule of law and reason. The use of this symbol was originally proposed to Frederic Bartholdi by French Freemasons.

Purchased at Liberty Island March 15, 1992
Sunday

The Statue of Liberty by the light of a full moon.

PHOTO CREDITS:

Bart Barlow/Envision: Inside back flap, inside back cover bottom right, 35 bottom. Bartholdi Museum, Colmar, France, reproduction by Christian Kempf: 11 top, 12 bottom, 15, 21. Dan Cornish/Esto:10 top, 42 bottom. Jack Deutsch/Visions: 32. Jeffrey Eger/Visions: 31 left, top right and bottom right. Brian Feeney/Statue of Liberty Monument: 44-45. Simon Feldman/Envision: 6, 36 right, 38. Tim Gibson/Envision: 2-3. Mark Greenberg/Visions: 20-21, 40. Brad Hill/Media Photo Group: 48 bottom. Evelyn Hill, Inc.: 42 top, 48 top. Historical Society of Pennsylvania: 23 bottom. Michael J. Howell/Envision: 8, 11 bottom. Michael Kingsford/ Envision: 29. Joseph Kugielsky: inside back cover top right, 13, 16, 28, 34 top and bottom, 35 top. Frank La Bua/Envision: 5. Library of Congress: 18, 43, 45 bottom, 46. M. Long/Envision: front flap. Melabee M. Miller/Envision: 4, 36 left, 47, inside back cover left, back cover. Museum of the City of New York: 14, 24, 27 top. National Park Service/ Statue of Liberty National Monument: 10 bottom, 12 top, 26, 30. New-York Historical Society: 27 bottom. New York Public Library: 19 top and bottom, 22, 23 top, 45 top. Jon Ortner: Cover. Doug Paulin: 37. Jefferey Vock/Visions: 39. Irving Weissdorf: inside front cover.,

ACKNOWLEDGEMENTS:

Special thanks are due to the staff of the Statue of Liberty National Monument of the National Park Service, especially to Brian Feeney, Staff Photographer, for extraordinary efforts in compiling the photography of the Statue of Liberty and Ellis Island. For their patience and constant support, we thank Sue Pashko of Envision photo agency, Julie Ades of Visions photo agency, Christina Trimble of Metaform, Irving Weissdorf, Louise at Esto photo agency, Evelyn Overmiller and the staff of the Library of Congress, Ellen Belcher at the New York Public Library, Gretchen Viehmann at the Museum of the City of New York, Diana Arecco at the New York Historical Society, and also the kind staff at the Historical Society of Pennsylvania. We are indebted to Mr. Jean Marie Schmitt, Director of the Bartholdi Museum in Colmar, France for permission to use several photographs from the museum's collection, and to Mr. Christian Kempf for his swift and very fine duplication of those photos. And we would especially like to acknowledge the work of Bart Barlow, who wrote the original text for *Statue of Liberty—The Promise of America* , ©1987 Evelyn Hill, Inc., on which the present text is largely based. Finally, this book would not have been possible without the help of many individuals too numerous to mention; to all who gave of their time and energy, we, at Sequoia Communications, would like to express our deep appreciation.

Table of Contents

The lower Manhattan skyline at dusk. Though tall buildings have long eclipsed her in height, the "Keeper of Dreams" remains the visual and inspirational center of New York Harbor's skyline.

CHAPTER·1

A Great Gift Conceived

In the summer of 1865, the United States of America had just come through the four wrenching years of the Civil War. It had been a crisis that had threatened to destroy the Union and, with it, the ideal of "life, liberty and the pursuit of happiness." But the grand experiment of democracy in America had proven itself valid, and now the world watched as an adolescent nation came of age.

Across the Atlantic, at the country estate of Edouard Rene Lefebvre de Laboulaye, near Versailles, a group of French intellectuals gathered to toast the future of the United States of America. Though France was then still held fast in the imperial grip of Napoleon III, Laboulaye and his guests were all strongly opposed to Napoleon's regime and active in the movement to restore a republican form of government in France. The triumph of democracy in America provided a beacon of promise for their own ideals. Laboulaye, a distinguished scholar of American history, felt there existed "a genuine flow of sympathy, and a shared commitment to the principles of liberty" between the people of France and the United States. It was he who first suggested the idea of a monument to American independence. It should be built in America he thought, but it should be "built by united efforts, a common work of both nations."

One of Edouard Laboulaye's guests that summer evening in 1865 was a young artist by the name of Frederic Auguste Bartholdi. Then only 31 years old, Bartholdi had already earned a reputation in France as a sculptor of monuments (the tradition of honoring political and military heroes and events was quite fashionable and well-established in Europe at that time). The concept of a project of such scope and grandeur caught Bartholdi's imagination, and with the encouragement of Laboulaye, the idea grew into an obsession for the artist. Although it would take 21 years, the spark of that dinner conversation would one day light the torch of the Statue of Liberty.

However, in 1865 the politics of France prevented any active work on such a venture. Bartholdi continued to produce his monuments to assorted civic heroes, but neither he nor Laboulaye could risk outright defiance of Napoleon III. It was not until six years later, when Napoleon III had been defeated in the Franco-Prussian War and the new French leadership displayed strong support for a democratic constitution, that it finally became safe to gather support for a monument to American independence. Both Bartholdi and Laboulaye hoped that the great gift from France could be made in celebration of the United States' Centennial of Independence that was being planned for 1876. Laboulaye knew that the people of France needed a strong symbol of democracy to remind them of the success of the American system and to ensure continued resistance toward the idea of a new monarchy.

"Propose to our friends over there to make with us a monument, a common work, in remembrance of the ancient friendship of France and the United States," Laboulaye wrote to Bartholdi as the artist set out for America in 1871. "We will take up a subscription in France. If you find a happy idea, a plan that will excite public enthusiasm, we are convinced that it will be successful on both continents, and we will do a work that will have a far-reaching moral effect."

BARTHOLDI GOES TO AMERICA

By the spring of 1871, Bartholdi arrived in New York with the beginnings of a plan for the monument. But as he came into New York Harbor, it became a clear and definite vision. He wrote: *The picture that is*

Above: Liberty's strong features, at once vigilant and welcoming, are based on those of Bartholdi's beloved mother, Charlotte Beysser, who encouraged her son's artistic talents. Right: A portrait of Edouard Laboulaye, who conceived the idea of a strong visual symbol that would serve to remind the world that "Liberty lives only through Truth and Justice, Reason and Law."

presented to the view when one arrives at
New York is marvelous, when, after some
days of voyaging, in the pearly radiance of
a beautiful morning is revealed the magnificent spectacle of those immense cities
[Brooklyn and Manhattan], of those rivers
extending as far as the eye can reach,
festooned with masts and flags; when one
awakes, so to speak, in the midst of that
interior sea covered with vessels...it is
thrilling. It is, indeed, the New World, which
appears in its majestic expanse, with the
ardor of its glowing life.

In a short time Bartholdi created new
drawings of a great lady. Unlike his ill-fated
Egyptian model, which Bartholdi had
designed as an Egyptian peasant woman for
the entrance to the Suez Canal, this statue
was to be a classical goddess, carrying a
tablet of law inscribed in Roman numerals
with the date of the American Declaration
of Independence. She would wear a crown
of seven rays, signifying the seven conti-

*Top: Between 1867 and
1869, Bartholdi created
designs and models for an
immense lighthouse at the
entry of the newly built Suez
Canal, to be called* Egypt (or
Progress) Bringing the Light
to Asia. *Though this project
was never built, it served as
an inspiration for the Statue
of Liberty. Left: Liberty's
strong arms are said to be
modeled after those of
Bartholdi's wife, Jeanne-
Emilie. The seven rays of her
crown represent the seven
continents and the seven
seas.*

Above: A watercolor rendering by Bartholdi, circa 1875, showing his vision of Liberty in place on Bedloe's Island—the site he chose for the statue upon his arrival in New York Harbor in 1871. Right: Bartholdi's watercolor concept sketch for Egypt Bringing the Light to Asia. *Critics of the Statue of Liberty idea said that it was merely a revised version of the Egyptian concept.*

nents and the seven seas. At her feet would be the broken shackles of oppression. And she would hold up the torch of freedom for all the world to see.

Bartholdi made sketches of his vision situated on what he believed was the perfect location for the monument. It was a twelve-acre island in the middle of the bay that would provide an unobstructed view all around, yet it was small enough that it would not dwarf the scale of the statue. The island was known as Bedloe's Island (after the Dutch merchant who had aquired it in a land grant from the Netherlands in the late 1600s, when New York was known as New Amsterdam). The tiny island had come under the control of the new Federal Government shortly after the Revolutionary War and became the site of Fort Wood, a star-shaped masonry fortification built in 1811. By the time Bartholdi visited the island, the fort was no longer in use by the army, but Bartholdi decided it would make an excellent frame for the foundation of the statue's pedestal. Because it was on national territory and thus "belonged to all the states," and also because of its situation just inside the narrows of New York Harbor, Bartholdi felt that Bedloe's Island was the perfect "gateway to America."

With his sketches of Liberty on Bedloe's Island, Bartholdi traveled all over the United States, meeting with the prominent people who would later form a network of support for his project, and painting the magnificent landscapes he encountered— from the splendor of Niagara Falls to the majestic giant sequoias of California. He made important contacts with President Ulysses S. Grant, Henry Wadsworth Long-fellow, Horace Greeley, and a host of others, including the French society of New York. The vastness and the vitality of America impressed Bartholdi as much as the technological genius he found here. He seemed to feel that "his American" (as he was beginning to refer to the statue) would be right at home in this land.

The Americans, on the other hand, were not easily convinced of the necessity of such a project. In fact, there were many who thought it was impossible. Nothing on this scale had ever before been attempted; the technology was experimental; and the expense would be tremendous! Americans did not have the long tradition of monument building that the Europeans had. Moreover, the vast territory and diverse interests of the population made it difficult to generate enthusiasm for what was perceived as the wild scheme of an idealistic Frenchman. Some criticized the project as an artistic indulgence for the wealthy; they said that the rich New Yorkers should pay for it if they wanted it in their harbor. Philadelphia, after all, was the site of the Declaration of Independence; Washington was the seat of government. Why should the whole country subscribe to put up a monument in New York? Many others who listened to Bartholdi's amazing proposal were interested—but retained their Yankee skepticism.

When Bartholdi returned to France he carried with him several new commissions (one of these, a bronze statue of Lafayette, now stands in New York's Union Square), but he had little in the way of real support for the grand monument. The completion of the project in time for America's centennial celebration would be impossible.

Bartholdi conceived of Liberty as a classical goddess in Greek dress with the monumental proportions of the Egyptian Sphinx. Her magificent size, however, posed a huge problem for the construction of the statue. In this detail the separate copper panels of the curtain wall construction design engineered by Gustave Eiffel are easily visible.

Frederic Auguste Bartholdi: Shaper of Dreams

Bartholdi completed this terracotta model of Liberty in 1870. Twenty inches in height, it is one of the few early scale models that remain today in the United States.

The man who would one day create the beloved symbol of the American dream was born August 2, 1834 in Colmar, a city in the northeastern province of Alsace, France. His father was a prominent official of Colmar who died when Frederic was only two years old. His mother, Charlotte Beysser, moved the family to Paris where her young son would receive a classic education at the Lycee Louis le Grand. But Frederic Auguste Bartholdi was destined to return to Colmar and become the small city's premier citizen.

It was while vacationing in Colmar that the young Bartholdi first decided to become an artist. He studied painting for a time with Ary Scheffer, and then took up the art of sculpture with the famous Jean François Soitoux. At the age of 18, Bartholdi was commissioned to create a monumental statue in memory of one of Colmar's native sons, General Jean Rapp. This statue would launch his stunning career. Commissions for other public works followed one upon another—fountains, memorials, and monuments soon established Bartholdi as one of the foremost sculptors in France.

As were most of the artists of his time, Bartholdi was greatly influenced by the timeless wonders of Ancient Egypt. The discovery of the Rosetta Stone in 1799, and later the exploits of Napoleon Bonaparte, had triggered intense interest in Egypt and all things Oriental. The Pyramids, the Sphinx, and the other ancient monuments along the Nile had attracted a steady stream of writers, architects, and artists of Europe, particularly those of France, and Frederic Auguste Bartholdi was no exception. At 22, he made his first tour of Egypt. Mesmerized by "these granite beings," he was to write some years later that "their kindly and impassive glance seems to ignore the present and to be fixed upon an unlimited future."

The future of that period did indeed seem unlimited. This was an energetic, innocent time for a young man of ambition and ideals. The world seemed to be leaping forward with the inventions and achievements of the industrial age, and European values were evident all over the globe. Leaders of the countries of the Middle East, Africa, and the Orient were often in Paris to press for support for their projects.

In 1867, the ruler of Egypt, Ismail Pasha, met Bartholdi on just such a mission. France was offering technical and financial support for the building of the Suez Canal, but Bartholdi was offering to bring the Pasha everlasting fame with the building of a monument to the modernization of Egypt. The Pasha was intrigued with the prospect and encouraged Bartholdi to come up with a plan. So, when the Suez Canal opened in 1869, Bartholdi returned to Egypt laden with drawings and a model for a suitable monument to the Age of Progress. It was to be a modern colossus guarding the gateway of the canal, just as legends of the ancient Colossus of Rhodes told of a great statue that had held a flaming torch to light the way into the harbor of the Greek island of Rhodes for Hellenic mariners of old. Bartholdi envisioned a gigantic figure of an Egyptian peasant woman holding aloft a torch which would represent "Egypt carry-ing the light to Asia." Her headband was to be lighted so that she could also act as a lighthouse. However, the Pasha decided that the torch should become a water vessel such as Egyptian women still carry on their heads when they go to the well, an artistic change that doused Bartholdi's enthusiasm for the project altogether. The commission was abandoned, and Bartholdi left Egypt in disappointment, but the dream of building a great monument still burned within him.

One has to wonder whether our Lady of Liberty would ever have been created if Ismail Pasha had not suggested this change of design on the Egyptian figure. Bartholdi himself reacted with indignation to the suggestion that the Statue of Liberty was merely the Lady of the Suez Canal revised. But the similarities are undeniable, and there can be no doubt that the source of the inspiration for *Liberty Enlightening the World*, was the same as *Egypt Carrying the Light to Asia*. Yet, the allegorical figure of an heroic woman representing a lofty ideal and carrying some sort of symbolic object was a common device of artists of this period.

One such image, which probably in-spired Bartholdi's concept of Liberty, was the famous painting by Eugene Delacroix,

Frederic Bartholdi (1834-1904) from a portrait in the collection of the Bartholdi Museum in his native town of Colmar, France. One of France's foremost sculptors, he devoted 20 years of his life to his dream of building a great monument to Liberty.

Liberty Leading the People. It depicted a gallant revolutionary woman charging forward with sword in hand and the French tricolor banner held high. This painting was suppressed by the totalitarian regime of Napoleon III because it was considered too incendiary for the people of France. Never-theless, the image was in wide circulation among Bartholdi's circle of Liberal Republi-cans, and certainly must have influenced him in theme, if not in form.

Shortly after Bartholdi left Egypt, the Franco-Prussian War interrupted his career and changed the course of the French political struggles as well. Bartholdi enlisted as an officer in Napoleon's army, serving in Colmar. But his native city fell and was ceded, along with all of the Alsace, to the Germans at the end of the bitter conflict. Napoleon III was captured and his Empire overthrown in humiliating defeat, but this disaster turned the tide of public opinion toward a new democracy in France.

Finally, in 1871, the idea of a monument to American independence that had been inspired during that dinner party six years earlier could begin to take shape. America was looking forward to its Centennial of Independence, the French were building a new democracy, and Bartholdi was ready for his destiny. With letters of introduction from Laboulaye, he set sail for the United States.

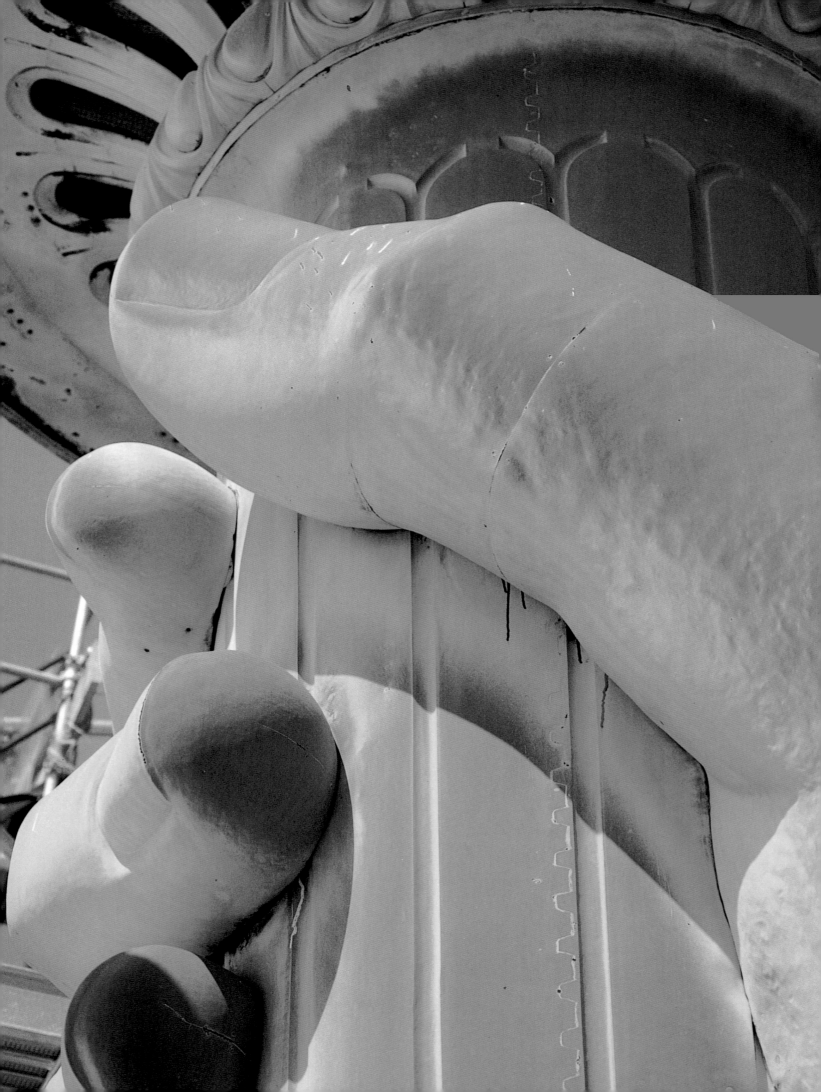

CHAPTER 2

To Build a Monument

For three years after returning from the United States, Bartholdi kept busy with other commissions and with refining the models for "his American." During this time, Edouard de Laboulaye wielded his considerable influence in France to increase enthusiasm for the Liberty project. By 1875, the *Union Franco-Americaine* had been formed to raise funds for the statue and work could finally begin. The great project took almost ten years. It became a stirring, if temporary, landmark of Paris as the statue began to rise over the rooftops of the surrounding neighborhoods. It symbolized the new feeling of liberty and patriotism that characterized the beginning of France's Third Republic.

Bartholdi, however, was more occupied with practical matters than with political ideals. The site he chose for building the statue was the Paris workshop of Gaget, Gauthier, and Company because of the reputation of its artisans, who had completed the metal work and roof sculpture for Notre Dame Cathedral and many other monumental structures. They were also experienced in the intricate technique of copper repousse, which Bartholdi had decided to use on Liberty (rather than the more common method of casting) because the size and material of the statue would make casting the pieces too heavy and expensive.

Previous page: The grand scale of Liberty—the colossal hand which bears Liberty's torch is 16 feet long. Above: Liberty was assembled between 1878-1884 in the courtyard of Gaget, Gauthier, & Company, rue de Chazelles, Paris. In a ceremony on October 24, 1881 the first rivet was driven into one of Liberty's feet by Levi P. Morton, U.S. Minister to France. The statue's head, which was completed first, looks on.

Repoussé is an ancient technique of pounding thin sheets of metal from the inside into negative molds that have been created from a plaster or clay model. This produces a close replica in relief; the finer details are added later from the outside. Bartholdi believed that the repoussé method would actually enhance the possibility for detail on a statue of such grand scale as Liberty was to be.

The fascinating process of creating a monumental sculpture—taller than any other building of its day—from a small clay model is the truly amazing part of the story of the Statue of Liberty. The original clay model for the statue stood only four feet high; from this the artisans of Gaget, Gautier, and Company would create a monument whose uplifted torch would reach into the clouds at the incredible height (for that time) of 151 feet.

This first clay model was enlarged to create plaster model nine feet high. The first plaster model was then reproduced again at four times its size, so that the third model stood at an imposing 36 feet high. At this point, Bartholdi made his final revisions, adding details to the face and hair, the folds of the gown, and the broken chains at her feet. When everything was perfect, a fourth and final set of measurements was taken. By using an intricate system of measurements, the last model was created in sections which, when added together, would produce one glorious lady.

For each of these final sections more than 9,000 measurements were carefully made and verified. In order to keep the proportion exact, 300 major points of reference and some 1,200 secondary points had to be determined on each section; six different measurements were taken from each point—three for the model and three for the enlargement. The ratios and proportions were carefully calculated from these measurements and then the enlargement was created by hanging plumb lines from the rafters of the workshop and connecting the points in a sort of three-dimensional dot-to-dot by means of thin strips of wood, wires, and supporting beams. In an incredible feat of carpentry, the proportions and details of the flowing robes and expressive face and hands of Liberty were enlarged again and again. When each wooden structure was complete it was then covered in plaster and refined.

Once the full-scale model sections were finished, repousse molds were made by building rigid wooden forms that closely encased the plaster sections. Crews of artisans then hammered thin sheets of almost pure copper into the molds. The more intricate shapes were painstakingly fitted into the molds by heating these sheets until they were flexible, then pressing and pounding until the will of the artist mastered the metal.

The decision to use the purest copper available, rather than a more expensive alloy, meant that the work could be done with pre-cut copper sheets which varied in thickness from about 1/8 to 1/10 of an inch. Because the statue would need to be shipped across the Atlantic, weight was of some consideration, but it was even more important that the material retain its shape and durability even in such massive proportions and against the winds and weather of New York Harbor. As it turned out, the pure copper skin of Liberty would withstand a century of salt air and Atlantic storms before she needed major restoration, and even then the damage was due more to the corrosion of her iron supports than to

Left: Molded copper sheets were attached to an iron framework extending outward from a central pylon of four iron post beams. The support structure was designed by Gustave Eiffel. Below: Gaget, Gauthier, & Company's workshop. Workers are pounding copper sheets into elaborate wooden molds; note the two plaster models of the hand and tablet, and the quarter-size model of the head at far right.

Friends in Liberty:
The Franco-American Union

Construction on the statue could not begin until 1875, when a democratic constitution was finally established in France with the founding of the Third Republic. At a grand banquet in November, 1875, Edouard de Laboulaye was named president of the *Union Franco-Americaine*. This organization was formed to publicize and raise funds for the project of *Liberty Enlightening The World.* The committee included some of France's most influential and famous citizens; many were descendants of the Revolutionary War heroes Lafayette and Rochambeau, and they wanted to maintain their ancestors' honor in the United States; others foresaw business opportunities which they hoped would come from their support of the endeavor; but most were simply caught up in the political fervor of the times.

Under Laboulaye's direction, the French committee sponsored special events and exhibitions, sold miniature models of the statue, and even produced a spirited opera, the *Liberty Cantata*—efforts which served not only to bring in the necessary funds, but to keep the ideal of liberty constantly before the public. It was important to the leaders of the new French republic that the statue be a gift of the people of France, and not another monument funded solely by the aristocracy. There was little cause for concern. The French people's enthusiasm for the statue continued undiminished for the entire decade it took to complete the project.

By 1876, the right forearm of Liberty and her great, symbolic torch had been completed in time for shipment to Philadelphia for the centennial celebration of American independence. Liberty's head and shoulders were finished in 1878 and went on display at the Paris Universal Exhibition, where visitors were charged admission to crawl up inside. Over the years, more than 100,000 individual citizens of France, and some 181 municipal governments donated to the cause. By July of 1881, a full four years before the statue was completed, the French committee was able to declare its campaign closed, having raised the equivalent of $400,000 to erect a monument to liberty in America.

However, the American Committee, as the other half of the *Union Franco-Americaine* called itself, was not even formed until January of 1877. It was headed by the well-known jurist William M. Evarts, and included such prominent men as the poet and editor William Cullen Bryant and industrialist Samuel D. Babcock, as well as nearly one hundred politicians, merchants, and philanthropists. The plan was that the French would fund the building and shipping of the statue; the Americans would fund the building of her pedestal, a task originally estimated at about $125,000.

It may be said that the Americans were just plain skeptical, or that the diversity and vast territory of the United States could not support a concerted effort as in France. Or perhaps the unhealed wounds of the Civil War affected their generosity. Whatever the reasons, the people of the United States did not rally immediately to the cause of providing a suitable base for the giant gift from France.

It was hoped that the 1876 exhibit of Liberty's arm and torch in Philadelphia would ignite the fundraising efforts in the United States, but the American committee met with a much cooler reception from its people than had the French Committee. Although the exhibit was extremely popular, there seemed to be a perception that the completion of the whole monument would be impossible. No metal sculpture on this scale had ever before been accomplished; the structural problems alone were overwhelming. Moreover, many considered the statue to be the useless plan of a wealthy aristocracy. Most Americans were reluctant to contribute to the project when they could never hope to see the statue in New York, as travel was more difficult and expensive in the United States than it was in Europe. It was also difficult to generate enthusiasm with a population unused to such civic subscriptions.

By the time the Statue of Liberty was complete and awaiting shipment in France, the American Committee had raised $180,000—mostly from elite art exhibitions and donations from such luminaries as P.T. Barnum and Andrew Carnegie. (Only $7,000 had come in from small donations of average citizens.) However, during the long campaign the cost of building the pedestal had more than doubled. In March of 1885 the American Committee published a desperate plea for more funds:

If the money is not now forthcoming the statue must return to its donors, to the everlasting disgrace of the American people, or it must go to some other city, to the everlasting dishonor of New York. Citizens of the State, citizens of the metropolis, we ask you...to prevent so painful and humiliating a catastrophe: We ask you, one and all, each according to [his] means, to contribute what [he] is able...[and] not to neglect this last opportunity for securing to yourselves and to the Nation an imperishable glory.

One who took up the challenge was the indomitable publisher of the *New York World*, Joseph Pulitzer. A blistering front-page editorial in the *World* denounced the failure of the wealthy sponsors of the project to come up with the "relative pittance" necessary to build a suitable home for the statue. He reminded the nation that this was a gift from the people of France, and urged the people of the United States to "respond in like manner. Let us not wait for the millionaires to give the money," he wrote.

Pulitzer promised to publish in his newspaper the name of each donor, no matter how small the contribution—and the pennies, nickels and dimes rolled in. From a group of schoolchildren in New Jersey came 25 cents; from Tillie Bradshaw of Connecticut, 10 cents; from a farmer on Long Island, two chickens. Whatever they gave, the *World* published their names in daily lists and covered the stories (some of which were of doubtful authenticity) of honest folk making touching sacrifices for The Lady. Meanwhile, circulation of Pulitzer's paper leaped by more than 50,000.

In just five months Pulitzer's appeal to the people raised the needed $100,000. Astonishing, when one considers the fact that it had taken the American Committee seven years to raise the first half of the funding. But now, and forever, the statue would truly belong to the American people.

Opposite: A stroll to see Liberty was a favorite Sunday pastime for Parisians, who were dismayed when the statue was finally dismantled for shipment to America in 1885. (Note workman at statue's feet.) Top: Liberty's head and upper torso on display at the Paris Universal Exposition in 1878. A winding staircase led to windows in the crown. Bottom: The statue's torch was on display in Philadelphia for the 1876 Centennial, and later at Madison Square Park. For 50 cents visitors could climb a steel ladder to the balcony.

Previous page: The Unveiling of the Statue of Liberty, *a painting by Edward Moran, depicts the 21-gun salute that hailed the statue's unveiling on October 28, 1886. Above: Political satirists had a field day with the disgaceful situation the United States found itself in when the great gift from France was due to arrive with the pedestal construction stalled for lack of funds. In this cartoon from* Frank Lestlie's Illustrated Newspaper, *the caption reads:* UNCLE SAM'S AWKWARDNESS—New Arrival from France, "Ah, Monsieur Oncle Sam! Escort me to my pedestal, s'il vous plait." Oncle Sam, "Well, you see, the fact is, Miss Liberty, we've only had ten years' notice to get the tarnation thing ready, so it isn't quite finished yet. But I reckon it will be complete by the time you get through the Barge Office."

Assigned to decide where Liberty would stand, General William Techumseh Sherman, knowing Bartholdi's desire for the Bedloe's site, chose it over Governor's Island.

On December 6, 1881, the American Committee chose Richard Morris Hunt to design Liberty's pedestal. The highly respected architect had a solid reputation as a designer of homes for the wealthy in New York and Newport. He had also completed several pedestals for sculpture. Richard Hunt's fee was $1,000 (which he donated to the fund to re-assemble the statue).

General Charles P. Stone served as the chief engineer in charge of the construction of the foundation, the pedestal, and the re-assembly of the statue. The pedestal sits upon a concrete foundation that grows up from within the eleven-pointed, star-shaped walls of Fort Wood. Stone used 24,000 tons of concrete in building the foundation and the pedestal, a total weight that represented, for that time in history, the largest single mass of concrete ever poured. Granite from Connecticut was quarried for the pedestal's exterior stone work.

To connect the statue to its base, General Stone sunk two pair of massive steel I-beams horizontally into the concrete; one pair deep down into the pedestal, the other near its top. Vertical steel beams connect the two levels. This anchorage system is joined to the statue's central support pylon via gigantic bolts. Liberty presents over 4,000 square feet of surface area to the force of the winds, requiring a linkage that is extremely secure. It was said at the time of the pedestal's construction that one would have to overturn the island itself in order to overturn the statue.

The pace of construction went in tandem with cash flow. The foundation was set down in 1883. On August 5, 1884, the cornerstone for the pedestal was laid. But it was not until the summer of 1884, after submitting a number of renderings, that Hunt finally hit upon a pedestal design that gained the Committee's approval. His concept was perfect for Liberty. The pedestal's massive bulk and 89-foot height would be broken up by architectural details that would give it flow and visual diversity, while not detracting from the statue itself.

But by March of 1885, just months before the disassembled statue was to sail for her new home, there was not enough money to complete the pedestal that Liberty would stand upon. This was when the Committee made their plea for funds from the general public… and when Joseph Pulitzer came to the rescue.

On June 19, 1885, inside 214 wooden packing crates aboard the French ship *Isere*, the statue arrived at Bedloe's Island, welcomed by a joyous flotilla, cheers, whistles, cannon fire, and music. On August 11, 1885 the front page of the *New York World* declared, "ONE HUNDRED THOUSAND DOLLARS!" The goal had been reached, the result of over 120,000 individual contributions. The republic, said the *World*, had been "saved from lasting disgrace." Before long, the packing crates on Bedloe's Island could be opened.

By May of 1886, the statue began to rise over the pedestal. A number of Liberty's 310 copper plates had been damaged or flattened in transit and had to be reshaped. Over 2,000 copper brackets, called saddles, were riveted to the interior of the statue's skin. They held in place the 1,825 armature bars that make up Liberty's iron ribwork. The saddles allowed for some movement between skeleton and skin, but, although asbestos cushions were used, the proximity of iron and copper also produced a major corrosion problem that would have to be addressed during the Centennial Restoration.

Workers, using 300,000 rivets, attached the 179,200 pounds of copper skin to its frame without using a scaffold. Hanging in mid-air from ropes, they were described by one writer of the day as "moving like industrious ants over the classic draperies and uplifted arm of the mighty figure. They reminded one of the Lilliputians swarming over Gulliver in the picture books."

On October 23, 1886, the last piece of copper, the sole of the right foot, was hammered on. At the total height of 306 feet, 8 inches, the Statue of Liberty was the largest structure in New York, and the tallest statue ever built. The statue joined the Brooklyn Bridge, completed three years earlier, as another visible triumph of the new industrial age.

A MAGNIFICENT CELEBRATION

When the great day arrived more than a piece of cloth obscured Liberty. Thick fog rolled off the ocean and rain drenched the streets of Manhattan; but neither dampened the spirits of the one million revelers who joined to make Liberty's official first day as

Enthusiastic Americans welcomed the white sailer-steamer Isère *to New York Harbor on June 17, 1885 with her unique cargo—214 crates containing the dismantled Statue of Liberty. Below: This engraving from* Harper's Weekly, *illustrated the laying of the pedestal's cornerstone, a six-ton block of granite, on August 16, 1884. Its copper-box time capsule contained, among other things, the calling cards of all the dignitaries present.*

an American joyous and memorable. On land, the massive crowds of celebrants formed "...rivers of life hurrying and sweeping through a thousand channels to the path of the pageant," wrote the *New York Times*. They watched a parade of 20,000 people pass down 5th Avenue and then Broadway to the Battery. All along the parade route, French and American flags fought the grey day with their bright colors; men and boys climbed telegraph poles, street lamps, and trees for a better view as 100 bands played and marchers marched. Veterans, military units, clubs, firemen, and student associations, among others, made up the three-hour-long procession. General Stone was the Grand Marshall.

The day was a public holiday, except for denizens of Wall Street, who worked. As a result, office boys, who wanted to join the fun, appear to have invented the ticker tape parade. The *Times* reported that the "imps,...from a hundred windows, began to un-reel the spools of tape that record the fateful messages of the 'ticker.' In a moment the air was white with curling streamers."

Out on the water, curtains of fog alternately revealed and obscured a jubilant fleet of crafts consisting of "everything that floats in New York, Brooklyn, or Jersey City," in the words of one visiting French journalist. The 250-vessel North Atlantic Squadron passed in a naval parade as tug boats, steamers, ferries, yachts, dredges, freighters, dingies, paddle-wheelers, and sailboats formed "a kind of floating archipelago of crowded islands."

The French and American dignitaries on hand made their way, after reviewing the parade, to the center of all this attention on Bedloe's Island. Congress had come up with $56,500 to cover the costs of the dedication, excepting refreshment. Private enterprise took care of food and drink, with great success, pleasing even the French.

The time for speech-making and dedication finally arrived by mid-afternoon. Above the speaker's platform, Liberty stood fresh and new, without the green patina that age and weather would give her. The statue, wrote the *Times*, was "glistening with rain, and rich in tints of brown and gray."

President Grover Cleveland, Ferdinand de Lesseps, Senator William M. Evarts, and other assorted luminaries were present on the platform. Up in the crown, Frederic Auguste Bartholdi waited for a signal from a young man on the ground, who was to wave a handkerchief when Senator Evarts

finished his speech. But the senator paused in the midst of his long-winded oratory and the young man took it to be the end; he waved the handkerchief and Bartholdi pulled a cord that dropped the French banner from the face of Liberty.

At that moment the festivities exploded in a euphoric cacophony. "Thunder upon thunder shook cloud and sea, the brazen voice of steam lifted its utmost clamors, colors dipped, men cheered and women applauded, the sounds of the sea were hurled back from the land, bell spoke to bell and cannon to cannon," reported an observer from the *Times*.

When the din of the whistles, horns, sirens, shouts, and cannon-fire died down somewhat, President Cleveland took to the rostrum. He had earlier called Bartholdi "the greatest man in America today." Now he spoke of the statue: "We will not forget that Liberty has here made her home;" he said, "nor shall her chosen altar be neglected."

The grand display of fireworks that had been planned for that evening had to be delayed for four days because of the rain. However, the spirit of the citizens of New York had hardly dimmed when, on November 1st, they witnessed a display of fireworks such as they had never imagined before. The *New York Times* description of Liberty's dedication fireworks declared that "it seemed that the earth had truly bounced from her peaceful orbit and shot pellmell into a shower of meteors."

Opposite: The seven rays of Liberty's crown represent the seven continents and seven seas. The famous viewing windows in the crown are the destination of many visitors. Below: The fully restored Liberty in the final rays of sunset, with her torch, and a new lighting system, displayed to full advantage.

Symbol of Liberty

Remember Your First Thrill of **AMERICAN LIBERTY**

YOUR DUTY-Buy United States Government *Bonds* 2nd Liberty Loan of 1917

This poster promoted one of the four "liberty bond drives" authorized by the U.S. Treasury Department in 1917-1918. Liberty bonds raised $15 billion, the equivalent of half the cost of World War I.

Just as Edouard de Laboulaye had hoped at the beginning of the long process, the creation of this powerful monument to Liberty had "a far-reaching moral effect." The soaring work has inspired many to speak with fervor of the ideas the statue represents. She has become much more than a formidable monument—she has become the premier symbol of the American ideal.

Since ancient times, Liberty had been portrayed as a woman. The version that Bartholdi created, most agree, bears a striking resemblance to one particular woman—Charlotte Beysser, Bartholdi's mother. To personify the idea of liberty, Bartholdi incorporated a number of classic, symbolic elements that speak a visual language shared by many statues throughout history. The concept of *enlightening*—giving light, as well as truth—comes across in the seven rays of Liberty's crown; which can represent the sun, the seven seas, and the seven continents. The torch, too, as carried by Prometheus, conveys the same theme. It is, as Laboulaye stressed, not "an incendiary torch, but a beacon which enlightens." The tablet represents law; the broken chains, liberation. As Laboulaye interpreted it, the statue "...tells us at one and the same time that liberty lives only through Truth and Justice, Light and Law."

But to millions of Americans, Liberty lives not only through Truth and Justice, Light and Law, but through Free Enterprise! One of the incredible aspects of this statue is how she can represent at once the loftiest ideals and the most vulgar commercial and political slogans, yet maintain her dignity and stature as an American symbol.

Through the decades, the image of the Statue of Liberty has been used to sell everything from war bonds to tobacco to underarm deodorant. During World War I, fully one third of the funds needed for the campaign were raised through the sale of Liberty Bonds. Then, after the war, during Prohibition, the Statue came to represent Liberty of a different sort altogether.

Still, by the time she reached her 100th birthday, the Statue of Liberty had come to represent all that is good, and noble, and free in the United States of America.

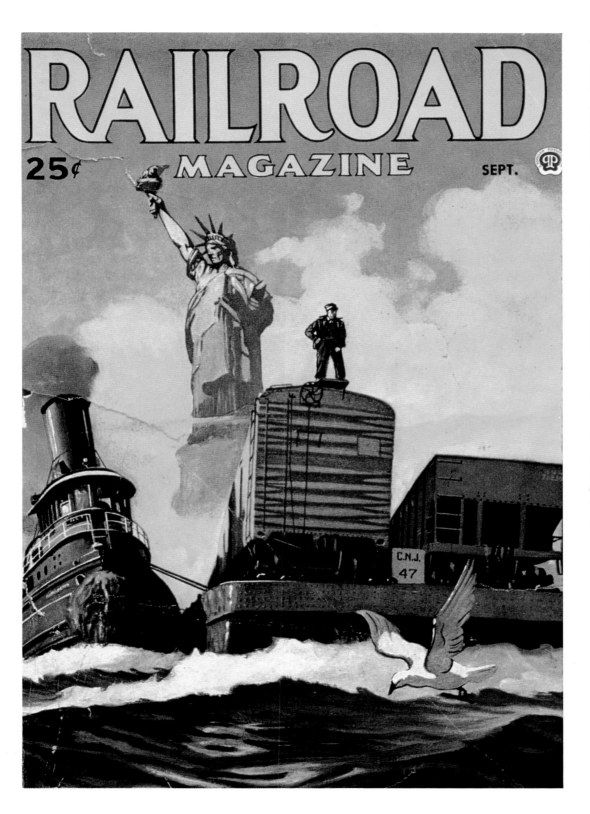

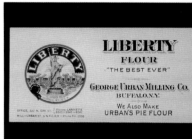

Universally known and admired, Liberty soon replaced Uncle Sam and "Columbia" as the symbol most immediately associated in the world's mind with America. The statue's enduring appeal has been used to sell everything from flour to pears, and over the past 100 years it has been adopted by publications and causes of all descriptions.

The Centennial Restoration

P resident Cleveland had pledged to remember that "Liberty has here made her home," and to protect and keep "her chosen altar" from neglect, but unfortunately, following administrations seem to have ignored those words. In the beginning, the Lighthouse Board, the Army, and the American Committee were the joint caretakers of Liberty, an arrangement that resulted in confusion of responsibilty for maintenance and repairs, as well as a divergence of priorities: the Lighthouse Board spent its interest, as would be expected, on the torch, as this was the aspect of the statue the board was qualified to maintain—but it also had the responsibility for the integrity of the entire statue, for which it was not as well qualified; the Army was in charge of Fort Wood and the military installations on the island, and treated the island not as a park or monument, but as a military base—esthetics were not the Army's primary concern; and the Committee took care of the visitors and operated the ferry system, but had nothing to do with the maintenance of the statue or the island. It was a recipe for ruin.

In 1902, after the commander of Fort Wood complained of the disgraceful maintenance of the statue by the Lighthouse Board, President Theodore Roosevelt turned the statue's maintenance over to the War Department, which installed the first elevator (in a shaft that was included in the original

Previous page: A blaze of glory during the July 4, 1986 gala celebrating Liberty's centennial restoration. Above and right: The world's largest free-standing scaffolding—a 300-foot-high, 300-ton aluminum structure—was built in 1984 at a cost of $2 million to surround Liberty during the year-and-a-half centennial restoration.

plan of pedestal architect Richard Morris Hunt). The War Department also made some necessary repairs to the statue and improved the island. Then, in 1916, after an attack by German saboteurs on nearby Jersey City that left many of the army buildings on Bedloe's Island severely damaged and some of the statue's armature bent (though the statue itself was not harmed), Liberty was given her first major restoration, just in time for her thirtieth birthday celebration.

The other major change during 1916 was to the structure and lighting system of the torch. Although the government had theoretically given up on the idea of the statue as a beacon, the Pulitzer family had not forgotten the role that Liberty played in stirring up patriotic zeal. With the global political situation in imminent peril, the *World* mounted a new campaign to renovate the torch to provide a moral beacon. The campaign brought in $30,000, and Gutzon Borglum (the future sculptor of Mount Rushmore) was commissioned for the job. Borglum had 600 pieces of copper removed from the torch and replaced with amber glass; fifteen 500-candlepower gas lamps were placed inside creating the effect of a huge, magnificent Tiffany lamp. However, the glass windows and the remaining strips of oddly-shaped copper could not be properly sealed and, in time, this became a major problem.

On October 15, 1924, President Calvin Coolidge renamed Bedloe's Island to Liberty Island and declared the Statue of Liberty to be a national monument. Yet, despite that special designation, when the National Park Service finally took over administration in 1933, both the island and the statue were showing signs of serious neglect. The Park Service immediately declared its intent to create a national park that would provide "a dignified and fitting frame for the celebrated statue." And over the years, it has made great strides toward that end. Today, following the completion of the Centennial Restoration, the Statue of Liberty and Liberty Island form a national monument that we can all claim with pride.

In 1981, the French-American Committee for the Restoration of the Statue of Liberty was organized to study the condition of the statue and evaluate the need for repairs and implementation. In the committee's initial diagnostic report prepared for the Park Service, it was determined that the statue was basically sound but that the supporting iron structure needed extensive repair and the torch would need to be replaced, among other recommendations. Funds for that work were raised, and the project was directed by the Statue of Liberty-Ellis Island Foundation, headed by Chrysler Corporation Chairman Lee Iacocca. Again, as in the past, private individuals were given a chance to contribute to Liberty. Over $295 million were collected, $69.8 million of which went toward the statue's restoration. The rest was allocated to a restoration of the Ellis Island immigration center (which will be complete this year for the Ellis Island Centennial) and to a trust fund for the future maintenance of both monuments.

To accomplish the overwhelming tasks of the restoration of the Statue of Liberty and Liberty Island, the Park Service and a proud and expert team of American architects, engineers, designers, historians, and construction workers joined together in a once-in-a-lifetime project to ready the statue for her 100th birthday—and for the next century. Appropriately enough, a team of 12 artisans from France would also play an important part in the process—as builders of Liberty's new torch.

The most dramatic symbol of the restoration was the largest free-standing scaffold ever built; rising 300 feet in the air around the statue and pedestal, the aluminum structure encaged Liberty for a year and a half. It was built to withstand 100-mile-per-hour winds; in 1985, Hurricane Gloria put it to the test with 70-mile-per-hour gusts which the scaffold weathered with no trouble. Because the statue itself can sway up to four inches in heavy winds, the scaffold structure came no closer than 18 inches from the copper skin of Liberty.

From this gleaming jungle gym, workers cleaned and repaired Liberty's copper skin. In all, less than one percent of the skin had to be replaced. The major changes visible from the outside involved the torch and the rays of the crown. Both were removed. The armature inside the rays had deteriorated badly. Once repaired, the rays joined the crown again. The old torch, however, would never be held by the statue again. Declared beyond repair, it came down on July 4, 1984, exactly one hundred years from the ceremony in France when U.S Ambassador Levi Morton accepted the deed to Liberty in the name of the United States. The old torch would serve as a model for the new torch, and then be put on permanent display in the statue's entrance hall.

From the beginning, the torch had been altered contrary to Bartholdi's original design. In 1886, two rows of portholes were cut into the flame, but the feeble light inside had not turned the statue into an aid to navigation as expected. A further change, in 1892, added a skylight with red, white, and yellow glass, and an 18-inch band of glass along the side of the flame. Bartholdi disliked both alterations. He died in 1904, and thus did not see the final, profound, transformation of his creation. In 1916, when Gutzon Borglum transformed the torch, it was the beginning of the end for the original beacon.

The new torch took shape in a workshop at the base of the statue. Using vintage photos, the old torch, and sophisticated computer studies for guidance, a French team of experts in repoussé worked to recreate Bartholdi's original design as closely as possible. The torch balcony was also replicated. Another French firm applied the 24-karat gold leaf to the new flame—a fitting continuation of the Franco-American cooperative enterprise of a century before.

Inside the statue itself, the major problem was a structural one. All of the 1,825 armature bars that make up the statue's ribwork had to be replaced. The potential difficulty with the armature was forseen at the time of Liberty's construction. The copper of the statue and the iron of the armature "do not agree together," a magazine writer of the day explained. "And where there is salt moisture in the air they seem to quarrel more bitterly than ever," he wrote. Liberty's builders used asbestos insulation between the two metals to counteract the "quarreling," which was, in fact, an electrolytic reaction. But the asbestos wore away over time, and massive corrosion resulted. The replacement bars, each carefully hand-crafted, are made of stainless steel. Teflon tape provides the modern-day insulation between copper and iron. The rest of the armature system—325 flat bars, 2,000 saddles, and 12,000 rivets—was also replaced, and in the statue's right shoulder the iron skeleton had to be reinforced.

Seven layers of old lead-based paint were removed from the statue's inner skin by a pressurized spray of liquid nitrogen at minus 320 degrees Fahrenheit. Two layers of tar under the paint came off after being blasted with 40 tons of commercial baking soda. Previous bombardments with other materials, including ground walnut shells, rice, and sugar, had met with no success.

Top: Liberty's old torch just before its removal, on July 4, 1984, 100 years to the day from the statue's deeding ceremony in France. Its windows, cut after Bartholdi's death, could not be properly sealed, and the torch fell victim to corrosion. Above: The new torch, a recreation of Bartholdi's original design, is plated with 24-karat gold leaf.

Liberty Weekend 1986

July 4, 1986 marked the largest pyrotechnical celebration in American history. Fireworks completely surrounded the statue during the 28-minute televised extravaganza known as the "Big Bang."

America gave a 100th birthday party for the Statue of Liberty in 1986 that shall not soon be forgotten. It was called Liberty Weekend—a 4th of July celebration so big that the weekend lasted four days.

The statue's restoration was completed just in time for the beginning of the festivities on Thursday, July 3rd. Liberty's new golden torch gleamed in the bright sun of a windy, crystal-clear day; the start of a run of magnificient weather that made up for the downpour during the dedication ceremonies in 1886.

The day began on the East River, with a parade of over 250 visiting sailing ships that were short enough to fit under the river's bridges. They sailed in the brisk breeze out of New York Harbor and past the Narrows, where they joined the tallest of the tall ships in preparation for the big parade on the 4th. At mid-day, 33 massive warships steamed into the harbor, stationing themselves along the parade route.

Thursday evening, with a golden sunset silhouetting the statue, the official opening ceremonies for Liberty Weekend began on Governor's Island, with President Ronald Reagan, President Francois Mitterand of France, and other dignitaries in attendance. "We are the keepers of the flame of liberty; we hold it high for the world to see," declared President Reagan in his remarks.

There were performances of song and dance, and Chief Justice Warren Burger, on Ellis Island, presided over a naturalization ceremony that, through a TV hook-up across the country, made 27,000 people new American citizens.

Finally, President Reagan pressed a button that sent a laser beam across the water toward the statue. It touched off a spectacular colored-light show that "unveiled" the statue and her new torch. Elegant and exuberant fireworks from a French pyrotechnical company closed out the program.

Friday, July 4th dawned sunny and warm. 30,000 vessels, from kayaks to the luxury liner *Queen Elizabeth 2*, filled the calm waters of New York Harbor. Over six million people converged upon Lower Manhattan, with millions more along the Brooklyn, Staten Island, and New Jersey

waterfronts. The morning began with an international naval review. Booming 21-gun salutes followed the passage of President Reagan, cruising down the Hudson River aboard the battleship *Iowa*. Streams of red, white, and blue smoke streaked from F-16 Thunderbirds in formation above. Then, great arching plumes of red, white, and blue water spouted from fireboats out by the Narrows—signaling the start of the daytime's main event: Operation Sail, 1986.

The great Parade of Sail included 22 majestic tall ships from 18 countries, and over 250 smaller sailing vessels from more than 30 foreign lands. As they had during the nation's Bicentennial a decade earlier, the awe-inspiring fleet sailed into the harbor, past the statue, and then up the Hudson, to the cheers of millions.

By nightfall the air was filled with electric anticipation as 32 fireworks barges, each with ten tons of explosives aboard, took up their positions around the tip of Lower Manhattan and out by Liberty Island. Called the "Big Bang," the 28-minute, two-million-dollar display that followed was the largest pyrotechnical celebration in American history. After witnessing the 40,000 projectile extravangaza of 1986, the *Times* quoted New York Mayor Ed Koch as

saying, "We expected the best fireworks since Nero set Rome on fire, and we got them!"

On the 5th of July, the statue was re-opened to the public, after having been closed for just over a year during the last stage of the restoration project. Circle Line vessels brought visitors from Battery Park, at the tip of Manhattan, to Liberty Island, just as they have been doing since 1953.

Liberty Weekend ended with a myriad of celebrations, including ethnic food festivals, concerts, sports events, a blimp race, and a grand finale closing ceremony with a cast of 15,000.

On the actual 100th anniversary of the statue's dedication (October 28, 1986), a crowd of 2.2 million people gathered along Broadway for a ticker tape parade. The parade, however, was for the New York Mets, who had just won the World Series. Out on Liberty Island, the statue's birthday was marked by a brief ceremony attended by about 1,500 people. During the proceedings the Statue of Liberty officially became one of 80 World Heritage Sites, joining such notable places as the Pyramids of Giza and the Palace of Versailles—places of lasting and universal value to the people of the whole world.

In 1886, the New York Times *said of Liberty's dedication fireworks show that it seemed as though the earth had "bounced from her peaceful orbit and shot pellmell into a shower of meteors"—a description that was even more apt for Liberty's birthday celebration 100 years later.*

Previous page: Liberty rests squarely in the center of Fort Wood, built in preparation for the War of 1812. The fort's distinctive 11-pointed-star shape forms the perfect foundation for the statue. Fort Wood never saw battle, and much of its original masonry is still intact. Top: A full-scale copper replica of the statue's face in the Statue of Liberty museum. Bottom: The statue's old torch, restored to splendor, is on display in the center of the monument's museum lobby.

the statue's interior structure in cut-away replicas, and marvel at the fascinating collection of Liberty memorabilia. The Statue of Liberty Exhibit begins with a full-scale reproduction of the statue's face, executed in shining copper repousse by the same French artisans who crafted the new torch. The statue's colossal scale is dramatically apparent here. A tall adult may stand beside this copper mask and be just able to look into one of Liberty's eyes. Another full-scale copper replica, of the statue's left foot, is on display beside a video screen that shows the repousse process the French metal workers used in making it.

The second half of the Statue of Liberty Exhibit is devoted to a look at the statue's first century. Her evolution into a symbolic beacon of welcome for arriving immigrants is powerfully evoked by excerpts of audio interviews from the Park Service's Oral History Project; a collection of first-person accounts by immigrants of their sightings of the statue, and their experiences at Ellis Island.

The notion of the statue as "Mother of Exiles" was both predicted and influenced by *The New Colossus,* a poem by Emma Lazarus, written in 1883. The poet was asked to contribute a poem to be auctioned as part of the pedestal fund-raising drive. Lazarus, a wealthy Sephardic Jew, produced a work inspired by her powerful reaction to pogroms in Russia following the 1881 assassination of Tsar Alexander II, and the resulting mass exodus of Jewish refugees, many of whom fled to the United States.

Originally placed inside the pedestal in 1903, a bronze plaque containing her poem is now a part of The Statue of Liberty Exhibit. The sonnet reads:

Not like the brazen giant of Greek fame,
With conquering limbs astride from land to land;
Here at our sea-washed, sunset gates shall stand
A mighty woman with a torch, whose flame
Is the imprisoned lightning, and her name
Mother of Exiles. From her beacon-hand
Glows world-wide welcome; her mild eyes command
The air-bridged harbor that twin cities frame.
"Keep, ancient lands, your storied pomp!" cries she
With silent lips. "Give me your tired, your poor,
Your huddled masses yearning to breathe free,
The wretched refuse of your teeming shore.
Send these, the homeless, tempest-tost to me.
I lift my lamp beside the golden door!"

The Statue of Liberty Exhibit ends with numerous examples of how the image of the statue has become not only a symbol of America, but also a popular icon—acting as a souvenir, advertising logo, and inspiration for folk art.

The American Museum of Immigration, one level above the Statue of Liberty Exhibit, opened in 1972. This engrossing facility celebrates the fact that we are a nation of immigrants. Murals, dioramas, models, arts, crafts, films and photos vividly depict the influence of 40 different ethnic and nationality groups upon our national identity. Many of the objects on display here were family heirlooms donated by individuals from around the country.

One of the most popular sections of the museum is a circular room that contains artifacts, including an organ and an inspector's desk, from nearby Ellis Island. The room leads to a massive, mural-sized photograph of a street scene in New York's Lower East Side, the destination of many during the period of peak immigration early in this century. The teeming scene is full of life, and the photo draws the viewer in to study the faces. The effect is riveting—causing one to feel the striving energy of people who came to the New World to find a better life.

Ellis Island: Gateway to America

Ellis Island Immigration Museum Directory

3

East **Treasures from Home**
Cherished objects brought from the Homeland

East **Ellis Island Chronicles**
300 year overview of the island's history

East **Silent Voices**
The immigration station abandoned

East **Restoring a Landmark**
Transforming a ruin into a national museum

Center **Dormitory Room**
ca. 1908

Center **Changing Exhibits**

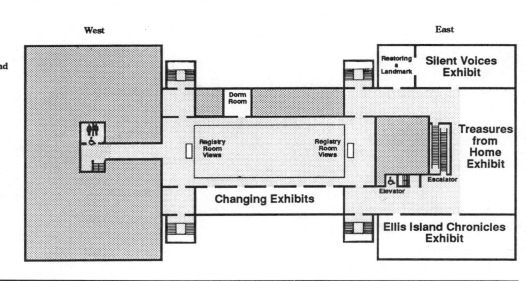

2

Center **Registry Room**
The historic Great Hall

West **Through America's Gate**
Processing immigrants at Ellis Island 1892-1924

East **Peak Immigration Years**
Immigration to the U.S., 1880-1924

East **Theater 2**

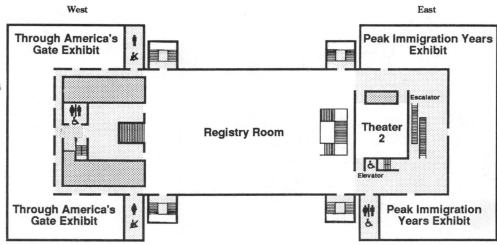

1

Center **The Peopling of America**
400 years of U.S. immigration history

West **Changing Exhibits**

East **Theater 1**

Center **Information**

East **Food & Shop**

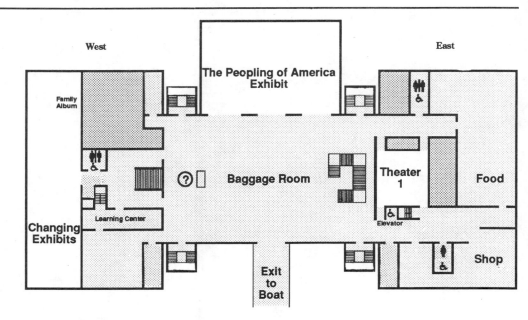

EATING & DRINKING IS RESTRICTED TO THE FOOD SERVICE AREA ONLY!
SMOKING IS PROHIBITED IN GOVERNMENT BUILDINGS!

ATT: SCHOOL GROUPS: CHILDREN MUST BE ACCOMPANIED BY ADULTS AT ALL TIMES
ONE ADULT PER EVERY TEN STUDENTS

From its very beginning, America has been the destination for those seeking freedom and economic security—a welcoming oasis for those fleeing religious and political oppression. The urge to live a better life caused the greatest wave of immigration in our nation's history during the late 1880s and early 1900s. One small island in New York Harbor was witness to most of it. Ellis Island, just a few hundred yards north of the Statue of Liberty, acted as America's main immigration station during the peak period of influx from abroad. Formally opened on New Year's Day, 1892, the island would welcome over one million people in 1907 alone. All told, 14 million immigrants were processed through Ellis Island. It is estimated that approximately 100 million Americans today are related to people who first set foot on American soil on that small island next door to the Statue of Liberty.

The main building on Ellis Island contains a massive two-story room filled with history. Called the Great Hall, or Registry Room, its vaulted ceiling is reminiscent of a cathedral; and indeed, its emotional power, for many, is equivalent. The Great Hall was where new arrivals waited in a kind of limbo between the old world and the new. There, and in rooms adjoining it, they passed through a battery of examinations that determined whether or not they would be admitted to the United States. It was, for most, a disorienting and fearful process—a wrong answer to one of the questions posed by an inspector could mean temporary detention, examination by a board of inquiry, or even possible deportation. So could a letter written in chalk on your clothes by a doctor—a code that stood for a suspected medical or mental problem.

In all, about 20 percent of those at Ellis Island were detained for one reason or another. Yet 98 out of 100 ultimately made it through the entire screening process successfully, some in as little as a few hours. Still, the fear of being sent back overseas—of being separated from one's family—caused many to call Ellis Island "The Island of Tears."

There were some abuses on the part of Immigration Service staff, baggage theft and

Opposite: The main building at Ellis Island, fully restored. Top right: Slavic peasants at Ellis Island, 1905. One woman carries her baggage on her head in the traditional fashion. Bottom right: This U.S. inspector is conducting an eye exam. He is looking for trachoma. The majority of immigrants rejected for medical reasons had this blinding disease.

the like, but, by and large, the immigrants were treated in as humane and professional a fashion as possible. This was no mean feat, given the volume that passed through daily, which sometimes reached over 5,000.

Restrictive immigration policies in the early 1920s slowed the flow of newcomers at Ellis drastically. The island subsequently became solely a detention center for those to be deported. During World War Two, it also served as a Coast Guard facility and as a hospital for wounded servicemen.

By 1954, all Immigration Service activities ceased on the island. Declared excess government property, it was essentially abandoned. Vandals and vegetation took over during a long period when future plans for the island were uncertain. In 1965, Ellis Island was declared part of the Statue of Liberty National Monument, and thus came under the jurisdiction of the National Park Service. In 1976, during the nation's bi-centennial, the Park Service began to restore the island, but the pace of work accelerated in the mid-1980s, with funds from the same generous donations that raised the great scaffold on Liberty Island. Soon, under the direction of the Park Service and the Statue of Liberty–Ellis Island Foundation, a small army was at work preparing the island for its centennial in 1992.

Ellis Island will reach its one hundredth birthday renewed, with its main building restored to look the way it did during the peak period of immigration. A museum and library, among other installations, will tell the tale of this very important gateway to the nation. Tribute will be paid, too, to all the ethnic and nationality groups that arrived at other places, during other times, to make America the unique synthesis of the world that it is. Plans are already under-way for a grand re-opening of Ellis Island later this year. The new exhibits will portray several different themes:

• *The Peopling of America*—a look at American immigration history over the past four centuries;

• *The Ellis Island Processing Area*—an in-their-shoes walk through the immigrant's admissions procedures;

• *The Peak Immigration Years,*

1892–1924—an overview of the immigrant's odyssey, from native land to adopted home;

• *The Ellis Island Galleries*—the story of the island itself, from early colonial times through the recent restoration, including a collection of artifacts brought by immigrants from the Old Countries. This area will also feature the Museum Houses, two study areas that will be open to the public and scholars by appointment;

• *The William Randolph Hearst Oral History Studio*—containing hundreds of taped interviews of former immigrants, staff and others;

• *The Library for Immigration Studies*—with documents and publications for furthering research on Immigration in the United States.

• *The American Immigrant Wall of Honor*—a memorial to those who passed through Ellis Island. It bears the names of more than 150,000 immigrants from 94 countries.

Opposite: "The Land of Opportunity" by famed photographer Lewis Hine. Immigrants endured terribly overcrowded conditions in steerage on their way to America. Above: Virtually abandoned after 1954, Ellis Island fell into disrepair. Restoration began in the late 1970s under the auspices of the National Park Service. The promenade of the Main Building appears on the right; the Ferry Building is on the left.

A Visitor's Guide to Liberty Island

Right: A view of the main mall at the entrance to the Statue of Liberty. Below: A Circle Line Ferry en route to Liberty Island.

Approximately two and a half million people each year make the memorable voyage to visit the Statue of Liberty. The monument is open every day of the year except Christmas (December 25th). This year Ellis Island will be opening for tours as well, and tickets may be purchased for one or both monuments.

Four Circle Line ferries operate on a regular schedule, leaving from Battery Park in Lower Manhattan and, in fair-weather seasons, from Liberty State Park in New Jersey. The first ferry leaves Battery Park at 9:15 a.m. and the last ferry leaves Liberty Island at 5:15 p.m. During the rare times when extreme weather makes passage dangerous, the statue is inaccessible.

Tickets for visiting the Statue of Liberty or Ellis Island may be purchased at Castle Clinton in Battery Park. The price includes the exhibit and round trip ferry ride. For up-to-date information on the Circle Line ferries' schedules, prices, and weather conditions, please call: (212) 269-5755.

Visitors should allow ample time to visit the monument and museums. In the busy summer season, four to five hours may be needed; in winter, allow at least two hours.